1 THE UNIVERSE — LOOKING OUTWARDS AND INWARDS

This chapter attempts to answer the question "What is Science?" We hope that you will read it with interest and be inspired with a desire to study science.

A scientist deals with *experience*—his first task is to account as far as possible for our common *experiences*. Why is the sky blue? Why do we sweat when we get hot? How do mountains come into being? Why is the sea salt? But to learn even more, the scientist tries to *enlarge and enrich his experience*. He looks at the stars not only with the naked eye but through a telescope; he studies the housefly not just by breeding it but by examining it under the microscope. He builds complicated types of apparatus to perform his experiments, and again enlarges his experience.

We are becoming technically more advanced every day—generally through the advance of science itself. As a result, scientists are improving our apparatus all the time, so that our range of experience increases. But some new experience may be startling and show them what they had never known before. Old established scientific ideas can always be upset by new experience and understanding. But the new experience must contain an account for the old. In science we never know what is going to happen around the next corner. So our ideas are always likely to change. That is why science is so challenging and why it is such fun.

THE SOLAR SYSTEM

The Earth is only a tiny speck in the universe. It is a **planet** of the Sun, a tremendously hot object nearly 1 million miles in diameter and nearly 90 million miles away from us. The Sun produces its heat and light by hydrogen-bomb reactions deep in its central region. The Sun has a number of **satellites**—planets—revolving around it, one of which is the Earth. Figure 1 is a simple diagram of the solar system.

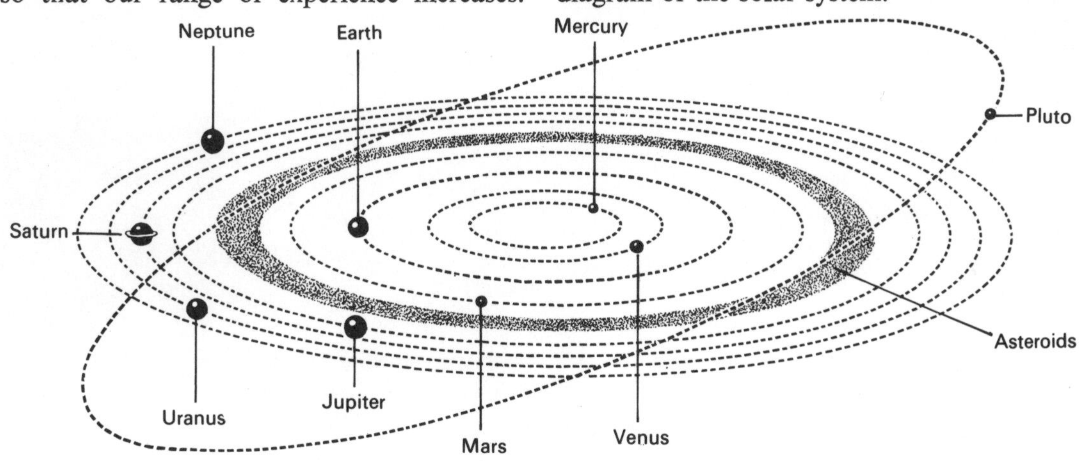

Figure 1 The solar system. Neither distances nor angles are shown to scale.

The Great Nebula in Andromeda-a system of some 10,000,000,000 stars, similar to our own galaxy. It is the nearest of the other great systems, yet its light takes over a million years to reach us This Photograph was taken with a 24-in. reflecting telescope. (Yerkes Observatory)

Figure 2 The Andromeda galaxy.

THE UNIVERSE
MATTER AND HEAT

Natural Science
An Integrated Course for Schools
UNIT A

Authors and Editors of the United Kingdom Project
PROFESSOR HERMANN BONDI, M.A., F.R.S. (Chairman),
Director General of the European Space Research Organization,
on temporary leave of absence from the Department of Mathematics,
King's College, University of London.
R. S. LOWRIE, M.A., B.Sc., D.Phil., A.R.I.C. (Co-ordinator);
M. HOLT, B.Sc.; A. B. SPIERS, B.Sc. (Econ);
HILARY SPIERS; C. BROWN, M.Sc.; ANN BROWN, B.A.;
J. D. NORTH, M.A., B.Sc., D.Phil.; SYLVIA CHAPLIN.

Illustrated by Lacey Hawkins

PERGAMON PRESS
Oxford · London · Edinburgh · New York
Toronto · Sydney · Paris · Braunschweig

CONTENTS

Many planets have their own satellites, or moons, revolving around them. Our own Earth has one moon, other planets have several moons, and only a few have none. The Sun, its planets, and their moons, make up the **solar system**.

STARS

There are many objects rather like the Sun, vast hot glowing spheres of matter. Since all the others are far further from us than the Sun they look only like tiny specks of light and we call them **stars**. Even the nearest star, *Proxima Centauri*, is so far away that light from it takes about 4 years to reach us. Scientists say the star is 4 **light years** away. A light year is the distance light travels in a year. Light travels at 186,000 miles per second or about 6 million million miles a year. So you may work out that the distance to this star is about 25 million million miles.

But even distant stars we can see with the naked eye on a clear night are still nowhere near the edge of the universe. When astronomers look at the heavens through large telescopes they see that our Sun is one of a large group of suns. We call such a vast group spinning in a space a **galaxy.** There are about 100,000 million suns in this group of suns we call our galaxy. Astronomers can also tell that the general shape of the galaxy is flat but with a bulging centre–something like a fried egg hanging in space! Our galaxy of suns is so large that light takes about 100,000 years to go right across it, and even 10,000 years to go straight through the thinnest parts—the white of the egg, as it were.

In Figure 2 we see a galaxy relatively close to our own, called *Andromeda.* This great galaxy has millions upon millions of suns like our own. It spins in space like a giant catherine-wheel. The small bright spots dotted all over the foreground are the stars of our own galaxy through which our telescope must look to see the distant galaxies. The big glowing spots are smaller galaxies.

We see what we call the "Milky Way" because of the fried-egg shape of our own galaxy. When we look at the sky across the fried egg and towards its centre, we are looking at a large number of the stars of our galaxy–so many that they give a milky appearance. This is the "Milky Way". When we look away from the fried egg's centre towards its rim or through the thin part of the "white", we see fewer stars so there is no milky appearance (Figure 3).

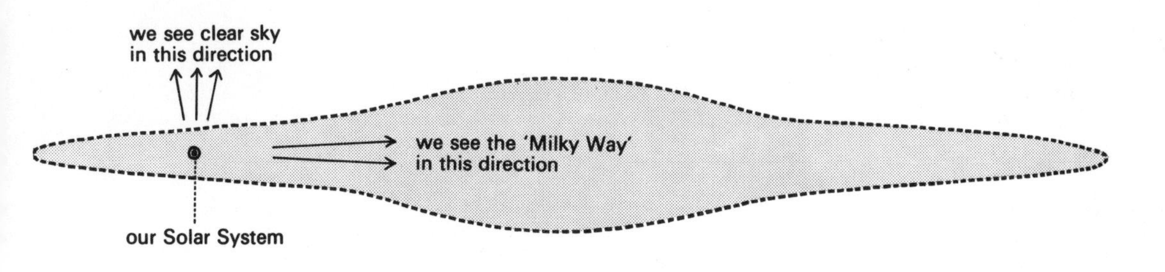

Figure 3 Our galaxy in cross-section.

GRAVITY

All the heavenly bodies of the universe are moving in curved tracks which often are nearly circular. Our Moon moves in an almost circular orbit around the Earth. Many artificial satellites also move in almost circular orbits around the Earth, and the planets move in circles around the Sun. Galaxies of millions upon millions of stars turn in space like huge catherine-wheels. Why is this so?

In the seventeenth century the scientist Sir Isaac Newton proposed one of the most famous and far-reaching laws of nature – his *law of universal gravitation* – that each object attracts any other object. This attraction is called the *force of gravitation*. We, as objects on this Earth, are attracted by the Earth and pulled towards its centre. This gives us our weight. Any object freed some distance away from the Earth is pulled towards the Earth by this gravitational force and falls.

If a spacecraft is to remain in space near the Earth it must move around the Earth all the time. Spacecraft must orbit the Earth in nearly circular paths. No satellite can stand still in space several hundred miles away from the Earth because it will be drawn towards the Earth by the gravitational pull and crash on the Earth's surface. Although it is under the action of the pull of gravity and falling all the time, its movement sideways carries it just far enough to ensure that the Earth's surface falls away beneath it all the time (Figure 4).

If all the suns of the galaxies were still, they

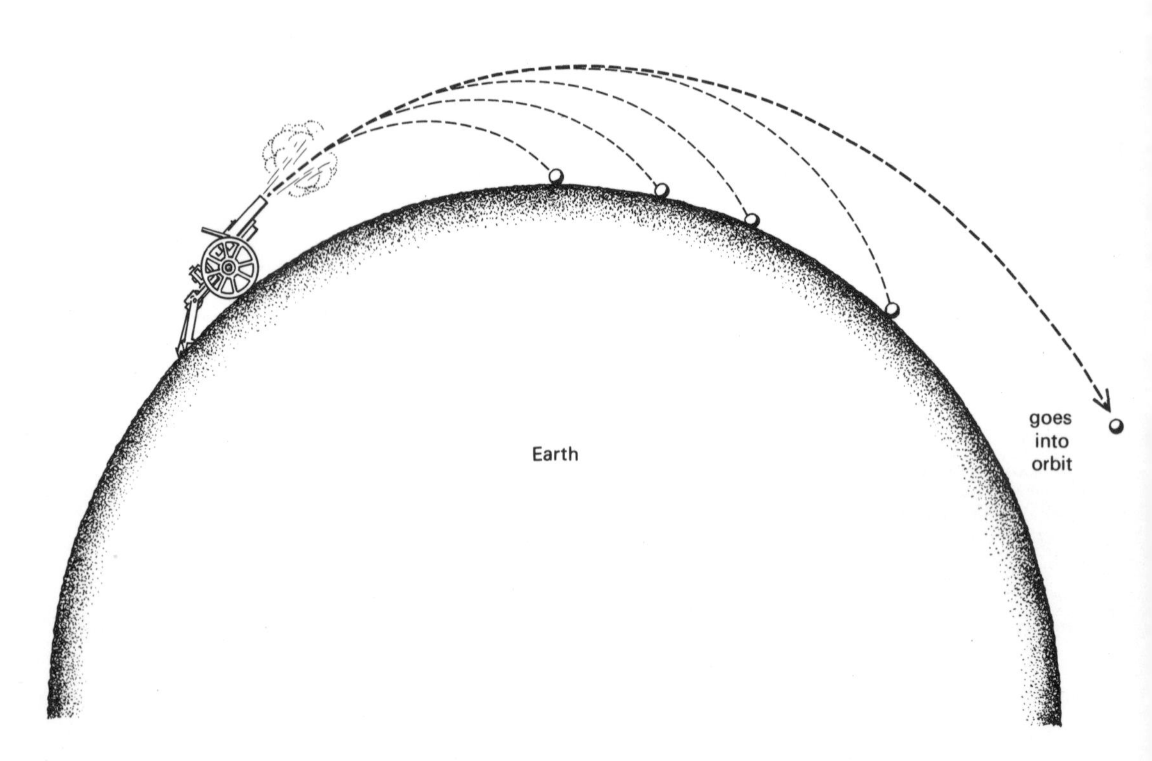

Figure 4 If an object is fired hard enough, it will never reach the ground, but will orbit the Earth.

would be drawn together by their gravitational attraction for each other and eventually collide. The continual movement of galaxies, whirling like giant catherine-wheels, prevents them from collapsing into a huge central star.

Our galaxy is only one of the countless galaxies in the universe. As far as is known, the universe appears to go on indefinitely.

THE PLANET EARTH

Geology is the detailed study of the Earth's crust. The enormous variety of rocks and other material the crust contains provides vital scientific clues to the whole history of the Earth's surface. **Fossils** – evidence of prehistoric life – trapped in the Earth's crust enable the geologist to trace the *evolution* of life on Earth. We see how the different forms of life arose, through the hundred of millions of years to the living world of the present, which contains more than $1\frac{1}{2}$ million different kinds of living things.

The evolution of life on Earth raises many questions. What is life? From where did life come? How does life work? What are plants and animals? How do they live, grow, and reproduce their kind? Answering such questions forms the science called **biology**.

ATOMS

A Greek thinker Democritus, living about 400 B.C., believed all matter was made of tiny particles that could not be split up. He called such tiny particles **atoms** (meaning *uncuttable*).

Not until the early nineteenth century did scientists begin to see Democritus was right. Today experiment shows that all matter is made up, as Democritus thought, of atoms. You will do many experiments and make many observations on the properties of matter. You will find how your observations can be explained by this *atomic* picture of matter.

SOLIDS, LIQUIDS AND GASES

Matter can nearly always occur in any one of three possible states – as a *solid*, *liquid*, or *gas*. In a solid the atoms or molecules are all stacked up in neat piles. Forces between them keep them fixed in position as if they were all tied together with little springs – as in Figure 5.

The atoms are always vibrating to and fro very rapidly. The particles' fast to-and-fro movement increases when the solid is heated. As the heating continues, the motion becomes so violent that all the little springs break, as it were. The atoms no longer stick together in neat stacks but wander around, never staying in the same position. The substance has become liquid. After more heating, the

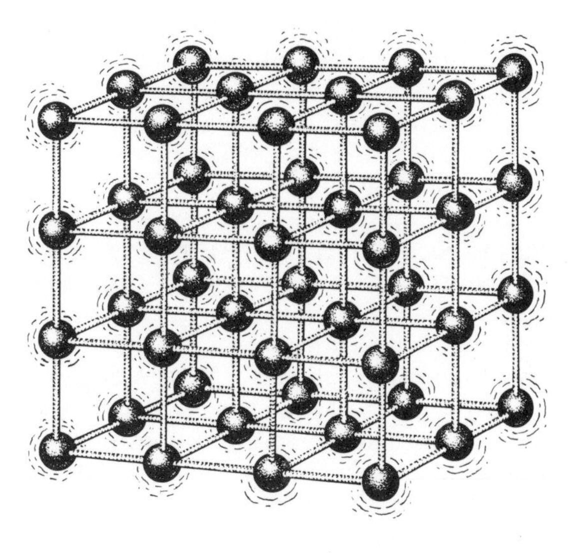

Figure 5 Model of particles in a solid.

atoms are moving so violently that they no longer stay together at all and fly off in all directions. The substance becomes a gas.

ELECTRICITY

Forces between the atoms in a piece of matter are caused mainly by electrical forces. The atoms themselves contain even smaller particles, called **electrons** and **protons**. These possess electric charges. Electrons repel other electrons but attract protons. Protons repel other protons but attract electrons.

Some matter in solid form, and in liquid form too, has a strange property: electrons can wander from atom to atom. Supply some force to drive them through the matter in one direction and we have an *electric current* flowing through the material. All electrical devices, so useful to mankind, are possible simply because we can make electrons pass through matter.

SCIENCE AND ITS USES

This chapter has given you a glimpse of some of the things scientists have discovered and are doing today. Scientists are explorers, driven by a questing curiosity to unravel nature's secrets. Their reward? A deeper understanding of nature.

Some scientists apply this new knowledge for the good of mankind – such as scientists in industry, space technologists, engineers, medical doctors, and computer designers.

To understand what science is about, you only have to look around. Your newspaper keeps you up to date on space research with instrument-landings on the Moon, pictures being sent back from Mars, and men walking in space. You may read about plans to bore through the Earth's crust – the Mohole project – or to create cheap power from atomic energy.

On a more homely scale, you watch television, listen to the radio, use the telephone, ride in a car or board a jet. None of these inventions was known a hundred years ago! These marvels owe their existence to the genius of a few scientists. You see the products of science in the X-ray machine used by the dentist or in the drugs prescribed by your doctor.

Science affects everyone – mother at home, the farmer in the fields, the foreman in the factory; and the surgeon in the hospital.

In the home, your mother uses scientific inventions such as the washing machine, the electric light, the gas stove or electric cooker, and detergents for washing.

In agriculture, science has given the farmer grain that resists disease and gives larger harvests of crops. It has also given him chemical sprays for controlling pests.

In industry, science has revolutionized manufacturing methods. The Industrial Revolution gave way to mass production in the motor-car industry, which was followed by automation. Steel rolling mills are now entirely operated by push-button control – a masterpiece of scientific automation. Petrol and oil are produced in fully automated refineries. Every year, hundreds of new and useful chemicals are created, such as the man-made fibres nylon and rayon, and fertilizers. The electronics industry is one of the largest in the world. But without the radio valve or transistor it would not exist!

In medicine, science has produced life-saving drugs like penicillin for killing all kinds of diseases and insulin for helping patients suffering from diabetes. Thanks to science surgeons can rely on such devices as artificial kidney machines, heart-lung machines, and the laser, the most powerful man-made source of artificial light, used for carrying out eye operations.

Work through these books, and we hope you will understand some of the things science has already discovered, and want to learn far more about nature. In this way, you will be able to grasp the major scientific discoveries bound to be made during your life-time. You may make your own contribution to science or technology and so help the community in which you live.

SCIENTIFIC METHOD

These books will show you a vital side to science – the *scientific method.*

By scientific method we mean, on the one hand, that scientists must *observe.* They must observe carefully and record their results accurately. This should always be done in such a way that others can repeat the observations and check the results. Only through constant checking and re-checking can the chance of errors be kept small. Only in this way can reliable knowledge be built up.

On the other hand scientists try to develop a *theory* to account for their findings. A good theory is one that fits all the observed results and makes them seem quite natural. They use this theory to *predict* the results of new observations. If these predictions turn out to be right, this is evidence that the theory has some value. If, on the other hand, new observations give results against the theory, then a new theory must be found.

The theory suggests new observations by means of which it can be tested. If an observation disproves a theory, then it certainly produces the need for a new theory and may suggest how it should be devised.

WORD LIST

atom
biology
electron
fossil
galaxy
geology
light years
planet
proton
satellite
solar system

QUESTIONS

1. There are nine planets. Name them. Start at the Sun and work outward to Pluto.
2. Name the planets that are much bigger than the Earth.
3. What is a galaxy of stars? Name two galaxies.
4. Why do not all heavenly bodies fall out of the sky or fall towards one another?
5. Some of the things listed here are solids, some liquids, and some gases. Sort them out. Water, stones, air, milk, brick, steam, ink, oxygen, ice and copper.
6. The Sun is about 93 million miles from the Earth. How long does it take for light to reach us from the Sun?

7. Work out how long it would take a spacecraft to reach Mars, 60 million miles away, travelling at 25,000 miles per hour.

8. From newspaper reports, magazines and books find out what major scientific problems are being worked on

(a) in Britain

and (b) overseas.

9. List the things in your home that were not known in 1900. Which of these are due to the discoveries of science?

10. Many scientists have made discoveries that have greatly affected our daily lives. Use your school library to find out the great discoveries made by the following men. Say why these discoveries are important to us:

(a) Michael Faraday.
(b) William Harvey.
(c) Wilhelm Röntgen.

2 MATTER AND HEAT

Suppose you were asked to list the most exciting things you would like to study in your science course. What would it contain? All your lists would probably have rockets, satellites, and space travel, and some of you might list the study of life itself, electronics, or atomic bombs. But very few would list ordinary, everyday things, such as water, air, wood or iron – things so common-place that most people would find little interest in them. But these are the things which first interest a scientist.

Science is mostly concerned with ordinary, material things – that is, with *matter*. Scientific studies show matter is as interesting and exciting as anyone could wish.

How can we find out what matter is like? Imagine for a moment that you are the captain of a tennis club. A new player comes along. Your job is to find out what sort of a tennis player he is. How would you go about it? Just looking at him and forming some impression of his strength and height may be of some help. But you couldn't say you knew much about his skill at tennis until you had seen him *in action*.

Now to find out about matter, scientists try to observe it in action.

How could you get matter into action? Is there any way to make it perform so that you could find out more about it? Make a list of the things that you could do.

Did you think of bending it, stretching it, scraping it, heating it, cooling it, adding acid to it, or hammering it?

Well done if you did, because scientists do all these things.

HEATING MATTER

First let us get matter into action by heating it. Place a few pieces of ice in a test tube. Gently heat the tube until the ice melts. Now stop and think for a few moments. Heating the ice has obviously caused a change in the ice, but how much of a change is it? The melted ice is the same stuff as the unmelted ice. It would be a simple matter to change the melted ice back to solid ice by taking away the heat that made it melt. You could do this by placing it in a refrigerator. Water can evidently exist in at least two **states**. It may be a solid, or it may melt to form a liquid. The solid state we call ice, the liquid water. When ice melts to form water or water freezes to form ice, the change is called a *change of state*.

Hold a cold watch-glass just above the mouth of the test tube, as shown in the last part of Figure 6 and you will soon see drops

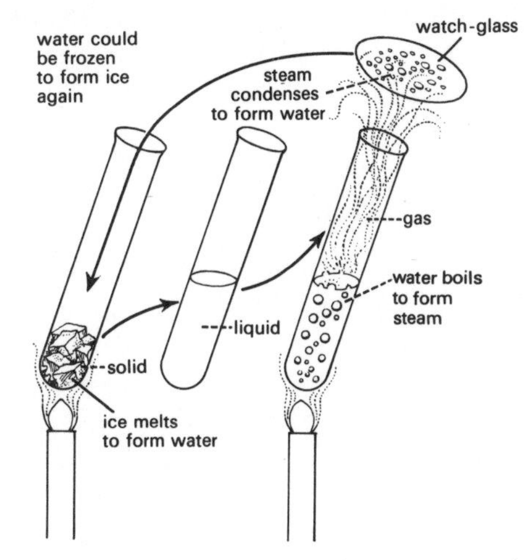

Figure 6 Ice, water, and steam are the three states of water.

of water forming. The water level in the tube is dropping too. In the clear space between the water in the test tube and the drops of water on the watch-glass, there is water existing in a third state. It is not a solid or a liquid, but a *gas*, or *vapour*. We call the gas form of water *steam*.

Water can exist in three states. Heat changes it from one state to another. The solid state melts when heated, forming a liquid. A liquid boils when heated to form a gas or vapour. Cooling the gas – taking heat away from it – causes it to **condense** back to a liquid, which may be further cooled until it freezes to a solid. All this is summed up for you in Figure 6.

Is water the only form of matter that can exist in the three states of solid, liquid, and gas? To find out is quite simple. Do the experiments that follow, and try to answer all the questions (Q.1, Q.2, etc.) from your observations.

EXPERIMENT 1.

Place some yellow sulphur in a test tube until it comes about ¼ inch up the tube. Sulphur is a solid, ground into a fine powder. Heat the sulphur gently until it melts. What kind of liquid do you get? (Q.1).

Continue to heat until signs of reddish sulphur gas appear above the liquid. Describe any other changes that you see. Has a change of state occurred, or has the sulphur changed into something different? (Q.2).

To find out, allow the test tube to cool. Examine the sides of the tube near the top, and the solid substance remaining in the bottom of the tube. At first glance, neither may look like sulphur. But a scientist does not go on first impressions. Examine the substance carefully, breaking open any solid lumps. You should soon be able to recognize what you started with! It too can exist in three states.

EXPERIMENT 2.

Some people use moth-balls to keep wardrobes free of moths. Moth-balls are made of naphthalene, a white waxy-looking solid. Place a few small pieces in a test tube and heat gently. Does it melt easily? (Q.1). What does the liquid look like? (Q.2). Does it boil? (Q.3). On cooling, what solid forms? (Q.4). Has the naphthalene undergone a change of state? (Q.5).

EXPERIMENT 3.

Place two or three black, shiny crystals of iodine in an evaporating dish. Cover the dish with a piece of filter paper. Stand a filter funnel upside down on the dish as shown in Figure 7. Place the lot on a pipe-clay triangle standing on a tripod. Heat the dish very gently with a low Bunsen flame. Quite soon vapours rise through the filter paper. What colour are they? (Q.1). As they cool in the filter funnel, what happens? (Q.2). How many states of iodine did you observe? (Q.3).

By now you are probably beginning to think that most substances can be changed into a solid, liquid, or gas, and this is not far from the truth. You can probably think of many other examples of substances changing from one state to another – melting lead, liquifying air, or melting iron.

In each example, remember, the change of state is brought about by heating or cooling.

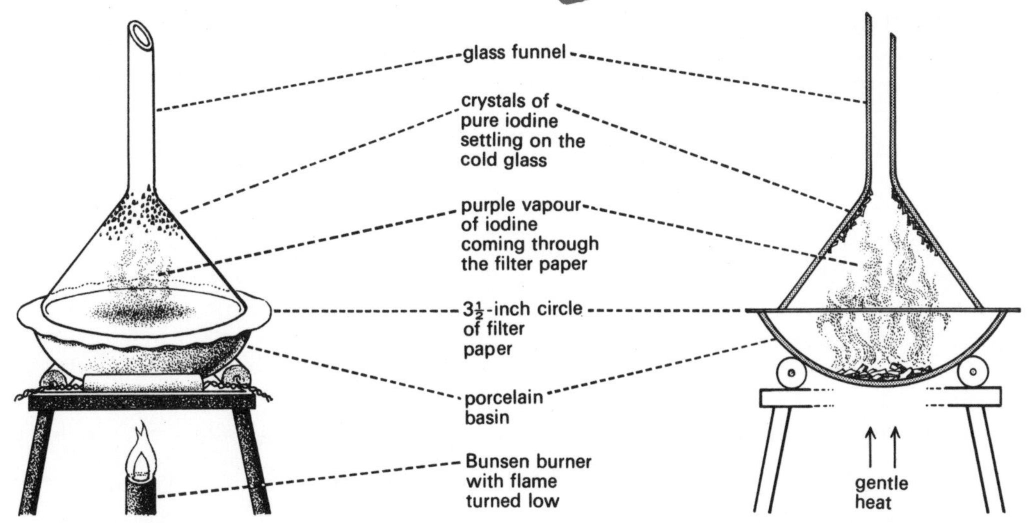

Figure 7(a) Iodine changes state rapidly as it is heated and cooled.

Figure 7(b) A convenient way of drawing apparatus in cross-section.

COMPRESSING MATTER

How can we squeeze a gas? A bicycle pump will do very well to find out about matter's ability to be squeezed, its **compressibility**. Better still use a plastic syringe.

EXPERIMENT 4.

Place your finger firmly over the hole in the end of the pump or syringe. Push the plunger in to compress the gas inside.

What do you notice? (Q.1).

As long as none of the air in the pump escapes, you can compress it a little. But can you compress it further? (Q.2.). Fill the pump with some other gas, such as town gas. Does the same thing happen? (Q.3).

Can you explain this behaviour of gases? Can you offer an explanation that might do? Think about it before reading on.

PARTICLES OF MATTER

A gas can be squeezed into a smaller space. So it seems a gas can also be spread out. This suggests that a gas consists of "lumps" of matter, with space between the lumps. If a gas is like this, it explains what happens when it is compressed. As we compress the gas, the lumps are forced closer together. The closer the lumps get, the more frequently do they bump into each other and into the walls and so try to push the walls out. Hence it becomes more difficult to compress the gas. We will call the lumps of matter in a gas particles.

You can use a syringe to find out if liquids are compressible. Water is a convenient liquid to use, but you can test paraffin, oil or any other liquid.

EXPERIMENT 5.

Fill the syringe with the liquid, making sure there is no air in it. Place your finger over the end and push on the handle. What do you notice this time? (Q.1).

No matter how hard you push, the water cannot be squeezed. It is just about impossible to compress it. We know that solids have shapes, which they keep unless we hammer them, bend them, or do something else to them to change their shape. On the other hand, liquids do not have shapes of their own. They take the shape of the container they are in. We know too that liquids can be poured, and that if they are spilt they will spread out.

How can our particle picture of matter explain these *differences* between solids and liquids?

Think of the particles of a solid as being joined to one another so that they cannot move past one another. This explains why solids have definite shapes. But think of the particles in a liquid as being freer to move, so that they can move past each other and take up different positions. This accounts for a liquid taking the shape of its container and for the fact that it can be poured.

Our particle picture is now just a little more complicated. Now we picture a gas as made up of particles spread well apart; a liquid as particles in contact, but able to move past one another; and a solid as particles in contact and held firmly in position.

Can this picture explain what happens during a change of state? When a solid melts, the particles must be broken away from one another so that they can move more freely. When a liquid boils, the particles must leave the liquid and move away from it, thus forming a gas. Our simple picture does not yet explain how heating solids and liquids cause these changes. So we may have to make still further changes to the picture to make it more useful. Let us use again our trick of putting matter into action to find out what changes may be needed.

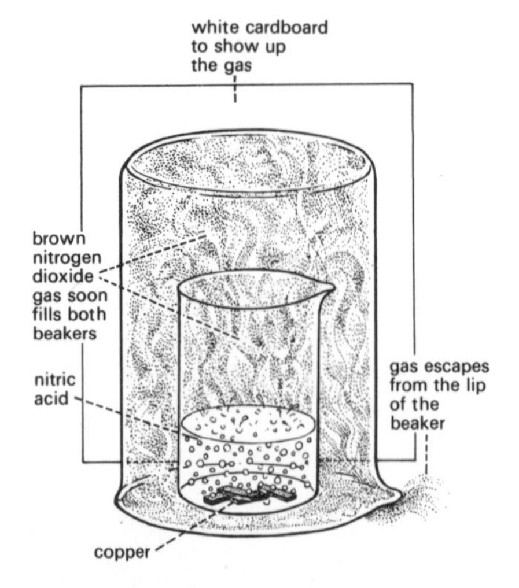

Figure 8 Brown fumes of nitrogen dioxide gas move of their own accord. They spread rapidly from the place where they are formed.

DIFFUSION

EXPERIMENT 6.

(*This experiment should be done by the teacher.*) Into a small beaker place a few pieces of copper. Pour a few drops of concentrated nitric acid on the copper. Immediately cover the beaker and its contents with a larger beaker. Look at Figure 8 to see how to do this.

The copper and nitric acid react, forming brown fumes of a gas called nitrogen dioxide. Watch carefully to see what happens to the gas. It might help to stand a piece of white paper or cardboard behind the beakers. After a short time, the brown gas fills the first beaker, overflows it, fills all the space in the second beaker, and escapes through the lip of the larger one. But it does not stop there. Gradually it spreads out from the beaker lip, spreading across the bench. After a short time, it will have travelled some distance from the original copper and acid mixture. Think about this. It is quite amazing. How can our particle picture cope with this strange behaviour of nitrogen dioxide?

Before beginning to explain what happens to nitrogen dioxide, try something else. You might do it in your classroom. Place a bottle of scent in the centre of the room. Close all doors and windows to stop air currents. Make sure everyone in the class sits with eyes closed. Someone take the stopper from the bottle. As each of you in the room smells the scent, put up your hands and open your eyes.

Like the nitrogen dioxide, the scent spreads rapidly to all parts of the room. It travels outwards, upwards, and downwards. In every direction it appears to spread at about the same rate.

There are many other similar examples. The smell of a cigar is soon noticed well away from the person smoking it. The smell of freshly cooked cakes will bring hungry girls and boys from great distances!

EXPERIMENT 7.

Place a piece of glass tubing in some copper nitrate solution. Put your finger over the end of the tubing. By keeping your finger there, remove some of the solution. Gently place the tube, with its solution, in a test tube of water. Take your finger away to let the liquid run out of the tubing underneath the water. Leave the glass tube standing on the bottom of the test tube, because you must not disturb the water.

If you have done this very carefully, you should have a blue layer underneath the clear water. Do not disturb the test tube, but watch carefully to see what happens. Can you see any change after half an hour? (Q.1). After several hours? (Q.2). How long did you have to wait for no further change to take place? (Q.3).

Diffusion ot gases

This spreading of gases is called **diffusion**. We shall need to add some more detail to our particle picture to account for it. How can we do it? It seems clear that the gas particles must be moving. Since they spread in all directions, they must be moving in all possible directions. As they move they collide with one another and bounce off any objects in the way. In fact, this colliding and bouncing accounts for the diffusion of a gas.

We can explain the diffusion of gases by assuming the gas particles are in rapid and violent motion. They are constantly colliding with one another and so being spread further apart.

Diffusion of liquids

Do liquids diffuse? This is an obvious question to ask because we are interested in liquids as well as gases.

This experiment shows liquids do diffuse, but much more slowly than gases. This means we shall have to add something more to our particle picture of a liquid. Just as we had to think of the gas particles as being in violent motion, so too we shall have to think of particles in a liquid as being in motion. But particles of a liquid are in contact with one another. So they would be colliding with other particles more frequently than the particles in a gas. Thus liquids diffuse more slowly than gases. Picture the liquid particles as sliding past each other and often colliding with other particles.

Diffusion of solids

To see whether solids can diffuse into one another, scientists have clamped different metals together for many years. By very careful measurements they could detect a slight diffusion of one metal into the other.

Their experiments show this diffusion is extremely slow and slight. Rock layers remain separate for millions of years. This again suggests that diffusion of solids is slow and slight.

Because a solid hardly diffuses at all, we must think of its particles as keeping their positions. But this does not mean that they have to be still. A classroom of children may be far from still, even though none may be out of his (or her) seat. Children turning around or fidgeting in their seats often cause the teacher to ask them to sit still. Although there is no moving from one place to another, there may be plenty of motion.

Scientists picture solids as something like a fidgety class. While the particles keep their positions, they just will not keep still, but constantly jiggle about, or vibrate. They have had to add this idea to the particle picture of a solid for reasons you will learn about later. We shall include this idea to give us a more complete picture.

Let us stand back and have a look at our ideas about matter:

> A solid is made up of particles almost touching one another, keeping the same positions but constantly vibrating.
>
> A liquid is made up of particles, very close together, but moving past one another. Frequently some of the particles collide.
>
> A gas is made up of particles, spaced well apart, moving violently in all directions and often colliding together.

Figure 9 shows these ideas in diagram form.

WHAT HAPPENS DURING CHANGE OF STATE?

When a solid melts there must be quite a change in the arrangement of its particles. From being vibrating particles arranged in an orderly way, they become particles that move about in a disordered way. Similarly, when a liquid boils, the particles move about more violently as they change to the gaseous state. How does heating a substance bring about these changes? It seems that heat must increase the motion of the particles. Can we test this idea? If heat does increase the motion of the particles, then hot materials do diffuse more quickly than cold ones.

The following experiment might give an answer to this problem.

EXPERIMENT 8.

Into each of two test tubes pour some warm gelatin solution. Follow the directions on the packet to make up this gelatin. The tubes should be about half full of the solution. Stand them upright until the jelly has set. Make up a coloured solution by dissolving some potassium dichromate in water and adding potassium hydroxide until the solution turns yellow. Pour about half an inch of this yellow solution on to the jelly in each of the tubes. Place one of the test tubes in the refrigerator where it will be cold, but will not freeze. Keep the other in as warm a spot as you can find, but not so warm that the gelatin will melt.

Examine the solutions after a few hours. Which solution has diffused further into the gelatin? (Q.1). Can you explain this using the particle theory? (Q.2).

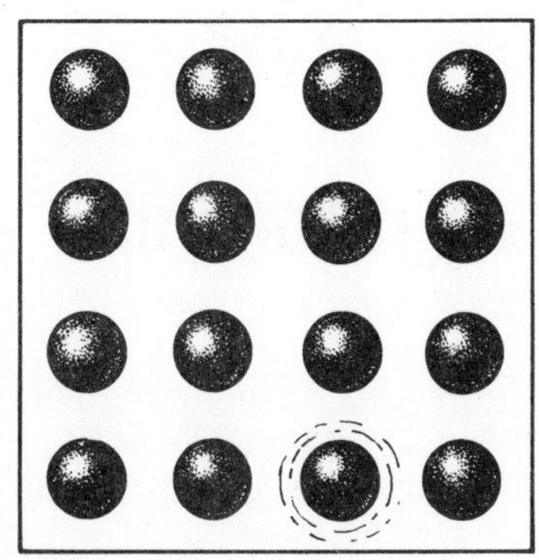

Figure 9 The solid, liquid, and gas states of matter. All particles are in constant motion.

This experiment shows heat increases the motion of particles. With this further idea, we can get a better understanding of changes of state. Let us follow the heating of a piece of ice and try to explain what happens in terms of moving particles.

We think of the solid ice as made up of particles that are vibrating. As the ice is heated, the particles vibrate more and more violently. At last, they vibrate so much that the solid ice shakes itself apart. It melts, and the particles move more violently still. Occasionally, a few of them move fast enough to escape from the others around them – this is water evaporating. Finally large numbers of the particles move violently enough to escape from the liquid and form a gas. The water boils.

When a gas is cooled enough its particles slow down and they come together as a liquid. The gas condenses. Further cooling slows the particles until they come closer together. They settle down into the neatly ordered arrangement of a solid. The liquid freezes.

PARTICLE MOTION AND TEMPERATURE

At some time or other most of you will have had the opportunity to measure **temperature.** Perhaps you have helped to make a weather chart and have read daily temperatures from a wall **thermometer.** Or you may have taken your own temperature or somebody else's using a clinical thermometer. During your science course you will often need to use a laboratory thermometer. You will learn how a thermometer works in Unit B, *Heat and Chemical Change.*

When we measure the temperature of an object, we find out how hot it is. Our particle picture of matter suggests that the hotter a substance is, the more violently its particles move. So measuring the temperature must roughly tell us how violently the particles are moving.

Temperature, tells us something about the **energy** of the particles in a substance. This is not a difficult idea for you to follow.

Think of the children in your class. Some are quiet and still. Others move about, work, and play games violently. These we say have lots of energy. Of course, children differ in size, weight, age and other ways. A large child moving fairly quickly may have just as much energy as a small child moving much faster. Substances differ in many ways too. We have to take these differences into account when we compare the temperatures of various substances. For the present remember this: heating a substance increases the energy of its particles, the substance becomes hotter, and we can see this by the change in temperature shown on a thermometer.

The melting point of ice is 32°F (32 degrees Fahrenheit). On the temperature scale more commonly used in science, it is 0°C. Here C stands for the **Celsius** temperature scale, sometimes also called the *centigrade* scale.

What happens when the particles of a substance stop moving altogether? The substance is said to be at the *absolute zero* of temperature. Nothing can be colder than this. Absolute zero is a very much lower temperature than the melting point of ice. It is 273°C below freezing point!

When we measure the temperature of a substance, we are simply measuring the average energy of its moving particles – that is, their *energy of motion*.

The sizes of particles

By careful measurements scientists have determined the sizes of particles of many different substances. They have found them to be extraordinarily small. The air around you is made up of countless billions of particles, too small to be seen, but in constant and rapid motion. The ink in the dot of this *i* contains millions of particles forever vibrating.

THE KINETIC THEORY OF MATTER

This heading looks most impressive and frightfully difficult. Yet you might be surprised to learn that, the important points of the kinetic theory are the same as those we have already worked out from our own observations! They are:

> matter is made up of extremely small particles in constant motion;
>
> in a solid, the particles are close together and vibrating;
>
> in a liquid, the particles are still close together but can move past each other;
>
> in a gas, the particles are spread well apart and move quite freely ;
>
> heating a substance increases the energy of its particles, making them move more violently;
>
> temperature is a measure of the average energy of each of the moving particles.

This is not a complete theory but it will do for our needs.

WORD LIST

Celsius
compressibility
condense
diffusion
energy
particle
state
temperature
thermometer

QUESTIONS

1. Name two solids, two liquids and two gases. By which of your senses do you know each exists?
2. A hot meal being prepared in the kitchen can be detected by its odour much more readily than a cold meal. Why is this?
3. Why is ether usually stored in a cool place in a corked bottle?
4. Describe what you understand to be the difference between the movement of the particles in water at 20°C and at 80°C.
5. What is happening to the movement of water particles during the evaporation of water from an open container?
6. Why does water evaporate more rapidly from the surface in a wide shallow pan than from the mouth of a bottle with a narrow neck?
7. The driver of a motor car pulls into a petrol station after a fast journey on a hot day. He asks the attendant to check the tyre pressures. What is he likely to find out about these pressures and can you explain why this has happened?
8. Describe what takes place in the movement of particles when air in a sealed container is heated from 20°C to 80°C. Would you expect the particles in this container to be farther apart at 80°C than at 20°C?
9. Describe the movement and compare the number of air particles in (a) a flat bicycle tyre; (b) a pumped-up bicycle tyre; (c) a hot pumped-up tyre.
10. A hot shower running on a cold morning makes the bathroom mirror steam over. This does not usually happen on a summer's morning. Why?
11. A moth-ball placed in clothing may completely disappear after some months. What becomes of its particles?
12. Name the changes of state involved in the following processes:
    (a) Washing drying on a line in summer.
    (b) Washing on a line in winter in a mountain area when the clothes are "frozen like boards".
    (c) Some water placed in a saucer vanishes into the air.
    (d) Some molten iron sets in a mould.
    (e) A custard is changed into ice-cream.
    (f) Water is taken into the air from the ocean and later falls as rain.
    (g) Some gelatin in water turns to jelly.
    (h) An electrician solders two wires together.

3 THE NORTHERN SKY

In Chapter 1 we discussed briefly the details of our solar system, our galaxy, and the universe of galaxies. We saw that our own solar system is a tiny speck in the universe. You were expected to take all this on trust. In the present chapter, on the contrary, we shall tell you of some simple observations of the heavens that you yourself can make. To understand and appreciate this chapter fully, you must go outside and use your eyes or a camera, to observe the skies for yourself.

Astronomy is the oldest of the sciences. Men learned to chart the sky long before they were able to chart the Earth. They knew the shapes of most of the constellations in the sky of the northern hemisphere before they knew the shapes of the countries in which they lived. Indeed, the methods originally worked out for charting stars were later adapted and used to chart places on the Earth. Astronomers were able to calculate the movements of the planets long before men could calculate the speeds of falling stones. And time after time, ideas first worked out in astronomy have proved to be useful in other parts of science.

THE CONSTELLATIONS

Most of us already know that the stars are arranged in a constant pattern. This is what people mean when they speak of the *fixed* stars. It is the *pattern* of the stars which hardly changes. But of course, as we all should know, the pattern moves *as a whole*, as the night goes by. It is as though the stars were all fixed on a rigid invisible framework. We know that some stars are millions of times more distant than others. Yet for convenience, astronomers often talk as though the stars were all fixed on a sphere, with us at the centre. This is a perfectly reasonable way of talking, when we are interested only in the *directions* of the things we see in the sky, and not in their distances.

The brightest stars seem to be placed on the "star sphere" quite randomly; and yet they fall into convenient groups to which men have given fanciful names. These groups are called **constellations**. It takes some imagination to see a great bear, a horse (Pegasus), a princess (Andromeda), and so forth, in the sky. But the imagination can be trained, and you may like to learn the names of the constellations in the northern half of the star sphere with the help of Figure 10. Simple star maps for both halves of the sky are shown in Figures 11 and 12. They show the constellations as you will see them, and not as they would be drawn on the *outside* of a star globe.

We said that the pattern of the stars appears to move as a whole. It appears to move, since we are ourselves moving. This movement can be observed in two simple ways. One way is to follow the movement of a single constellation by eye throughout the night. The other way, which is described in the next section, is to use an ordinary camera.

Most of us live in towns, where street lamps make it difficult to see the night sky. The stars that are most easily seen under town conditions are those that are highest in the sky. If you are reading this in the autumn term, you will find that such constellations as Cassiopeia, Andromeda, and Pegasus are high in the night sky. The Great Bear is not so high in the autumn sky, but it is more useful for our purposes. The part of this

Figure 10 A constellation map of 1540, by Peter Apian.

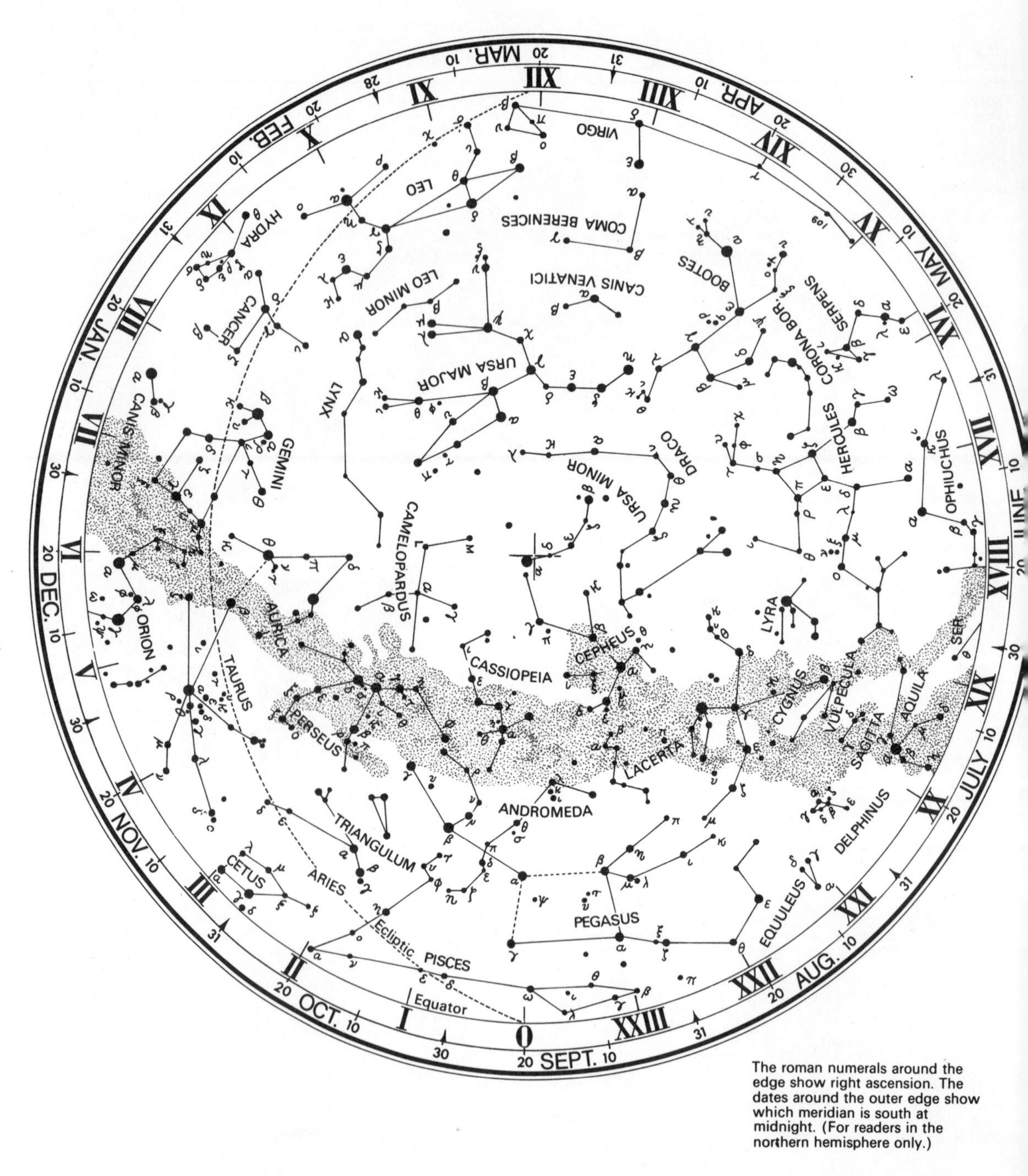

The roman numerals around the edge show right ascension. The dates around the outer edge show which meridian is south at midnight. (For readers in the northern hemisphere only.)

Figure 11 Stars of the northern hemisphere. Lines are drawn joining up the stars into constellations for convenience.

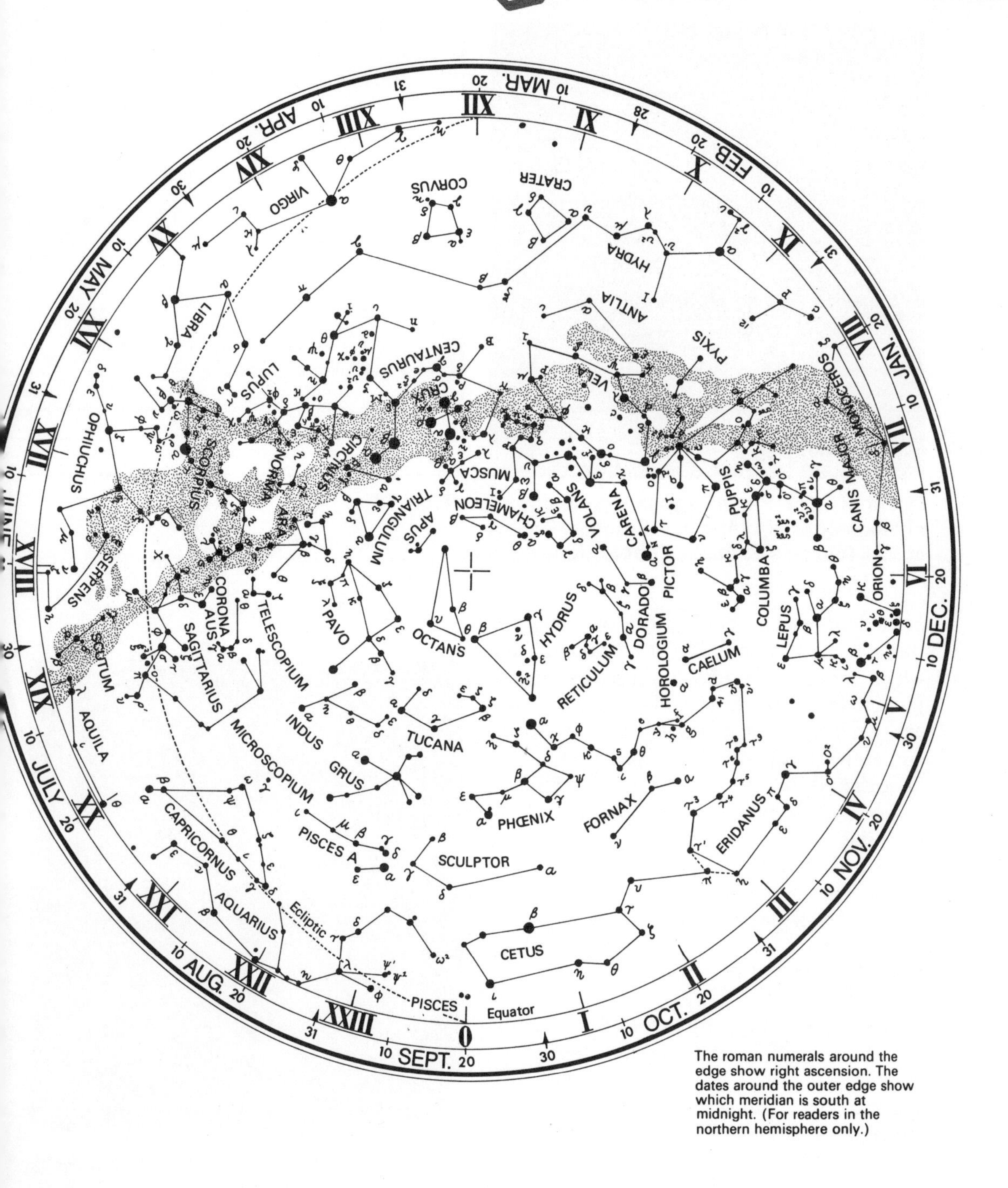

Figure 12 Stars of the southern hemisphere.

Figure 13 The Plough – seen upside down – photographed at 11.45 p.m. Exposure 60 secs at f/2.8 (film: Tri-X Pan). (Photo: R. Myers).

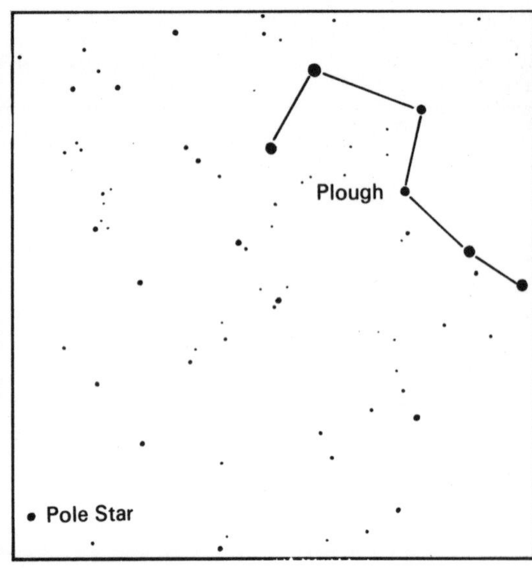

Figure 13 (a)

constellation that stands out most clearly is that which is often called the "Plough", but which looks more like a saucepan than a plough (see Figure 11). Pick out any two easily remembered stars, such as those in the end of the handle, and, when you are standing in a definite place, notice some landmark – a tree or a building – towards which they are pointing. An hour or so later, you will notice that the stars have moved a little. Taken together, Figures 13 and 14 show this movement. Notice which way the stars are moving.

STAR TRAILS

Perhaps you are surprised to find that the stars move at all, so let us examine their movement in another way. We shall use a camera, which will act both as an eye and as a memory. If we simply leave the shutter of a camera open, it will record not only the original and final positions for each star, but also all the positions between, as though each

Figure 14 The Plough taken as in Figure 13, but approximately an hour later. Can you find the Pole Star? (Photo: R. Myers).

Figure 15 The same region of sky as in Figures 13 and 14. The camera shutter was opened (at f/16) for 8 minutes, closed for the next 5 minutes, and opened again for 45 minutes. This clearly shows which way the stars are moving. The straight line across the picture is caused by a shooting star meteor). (Photo: R. Myers).

star left a trail in the sky. It will prove to us that the pattern of the stars is indeed constant as they move across the sky.

The photograph shown in Colour Plate C was obtained in this way. It was taken in Sydney, Australia. The camera was pointed to the Southern Cross, and the shutter left open for 42 minutes. Notice how the successive positions of each star form a continuous curved line. We shall call these lines *star trails*. You may at first find it hard to pick out the trails of the five stars of the Cross, but if you look to the upper left corner of the photograph, you will see the bright curved trails they have made, the four brightest stars forming the tips of a cross.

Colour Plate D shows how the stars in the Southern Cross move in about 17 minutes. Figure 15 is a black and white photograph taken in England with a simple box camera. What constellations can you pick out? This is the sort of picture you could easily take yourself. (Use the fastest film you can obtain, such as Ilford HPS.)

In taking the photograph of Figure 15, the star trails were interrupted for a few minutes, shortly after opening the shutter. By this means we can tell the *direction of rotation* of the stars. As we ought to have concluded from the photographs of the last section, they move *anti-clockwise* looking north. Can you calculate how long it takes the stars to make a complete rotation? (Remember that the longer unbroken part of the star trail corresponds to an exposure of 45 minutes.)

On Figure 15 there is one star so very near the centre of rotation that it scarcely seems to move. This is called the **pole star**. It is the brightest star of the constellation called the "Little Bear". It is a very useful star simply because it appears to move so little. Can you say why it is useful?

As already explained, the stars seem to be turning around us, but it is really the Earth that is moving – in the opposite direction, of course. The **axis** of the Earth, the line around which it rotates, must obviously point towards the pole star. What does the southern end of the Earth's axis point towards? Why are Australian navigators less fortunate than ours? (See Figure 12 and Colour Plate C.)

As you might have expected, each constellation starts out on the second night just about where it did on the night when you first observed it. Evidently it completes a full circle in about 24 hours. And if we assume that it moves steadily all the time, it follows that it turns through about fifteen degrees in each hour – about one twenty-fourth of the full 360 degrees. This should be roughly the answer you got in your calculation based on Figure 14. Strictly speaking, the constellations turn a full circle in about 23 hours 56 minutes. The reason for this will be explained later.

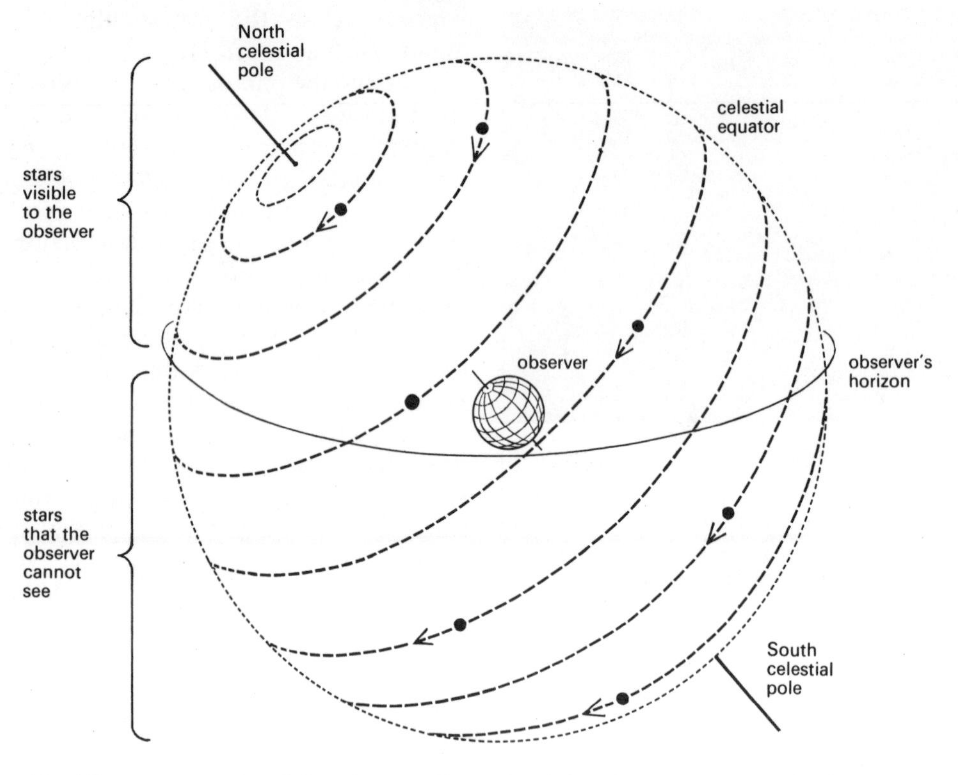

Figure 16 The movements of the stars as the celestial sphere rotates. Really it is the Earth that rotates, but this is a convenient way of talking. Can you see how the latitude of the observer decides what stars he has a chance of seeing?

THE SUN

Where does the Sun rise and set? Most of you would probably say that it rises in the east and sets in the west. Let us find out if this is true.

You must first find out the directions of east and west. Sketch the eastern horizon from somewhere near your home, marking carefully on your sketch the position of east. Now turn around and make a similar diagram of the western horizon. On the sketches mark the positions of the rising and setting Sun at weekly intervals, together with the date.

If you do this carefully you will find, as shown in Figure 17, that the Sun rises and sets in a different place each week. If you are very careful you will also find differences from day to day. This is something most people have seen, but have not noticed. They are often surprised to learn that the Sun does not always rise and set in the east and west.

Times of sunrise and sunset

If, when you were making the observations described in Figure 17, you also kept a record of the times of sunrise and sunset, you will have obtained evidence for something else, which you already know about. You will have seen that as summer approaches and the Sun appears to move northward, the Sun is in the sky for a longer time than it is in

Colour Plate A. Venus setting over the Sydney Harbour Bridge on May 17, 1962. The first exposure was made at about 5.30 p.m. and subsequent exposures were separated by about 10 minutes. Each exposure about 4 seconds. High speed Ektachrome at f/2. Taken from Mrs. Macquarie's Point in the Sydney Domain Park

Colour Plate B. Venus and the moon setting over the Sydney Harbour Bridge on July 4, 1962. First exposure taken at 5.50 p.m. and subsequent exposures at 10-minute intervals. Each exposure 6 seconds. Kodachrome II at f/2

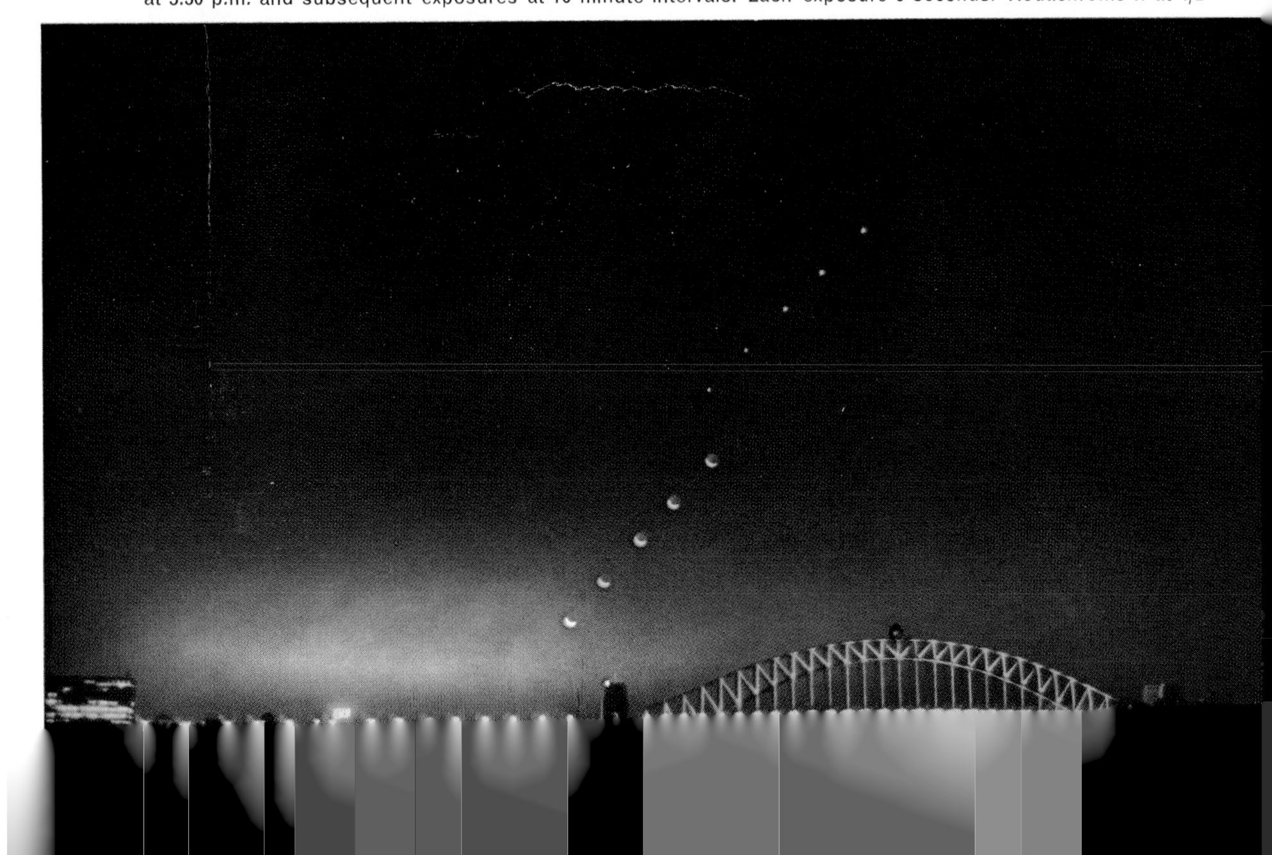

Colour Plate D. The Southern Cross, Alpha and Beta Centauri, and Musca. Taken at Wahroonga near Sydney on January 14, 1963, at about 11 p.m. Exposed for about 17 minutes on Kodachrome II at f/4

Colour Plate C. The Southern Cross, Alpha and Beta Centauri, Musca, Carina, and Chameleon. Taken at Wahroonga near Sydney about March 14, 1962; exposure began at about 8.30 p.m. and lasted about 42 minutes. High speed Ektachrome at f/2.2. Wide angle lens, field of view 63°. The almost straight track may be the trail of an earth satellite or of a meteor

north
south
the rising Sun
looking east
20th May
1st April

south
north
the setting Sun
looking west
1st April
20th May

Figure 17 As spring turns into summer, the Sun appears to move towards the north. Why is this? What happens during the other seasons?

winter. Daylight in winter is shorter than in summer, as we all know. At the same time, you might notice that in winter the Sun's path through the sky is much lower than it is in summer.

It appears, then, that although the Sun moves daily across the sky in somewhat the same way as the stars do, it has a northward and southward motion as well.

THE PLANETS

For thousands of years men have observed the planets, or "wandering stars". The planets earned this name because they move through the so-called fixed stars. They do so in a much more complicated way than the Sun. Instead of moving through the stars along a circular path, their paths are looped. (See Figure 19.)

For at least three thousand years men tried to account for the movement of the planets. Naturally enough, they began by putting the Earth at the centre of the universe. But a

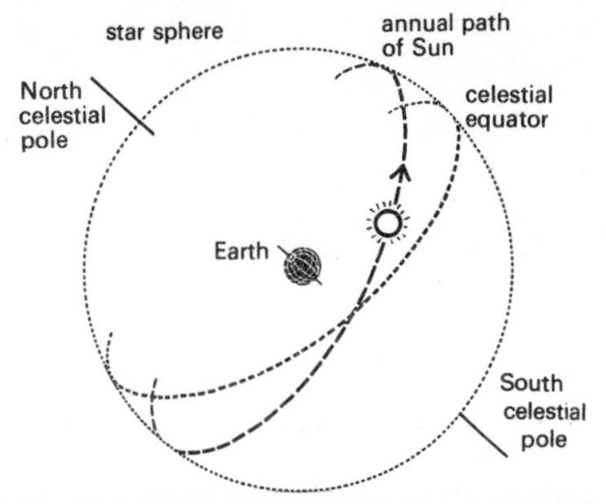

Figure 18 Diagram showing the path the Sun seems to follow through the stars. It takes a year to go round once. Notice that we have not drawn a horizon, and that we are not talking about daily movements as in Figure 17.

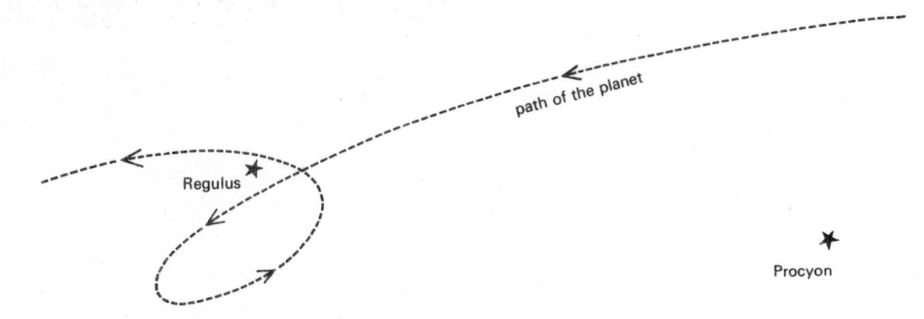

Figure 19 A typical loop in the path of a planet, against the background of stars. (The planet Mercury followed this path during the months of July, August and September, 1958. The only stars named are the brightest in the region.) Redrawn from *C. B. Isaac Newton* by Dr J. D. North, published by Oxford University Press.

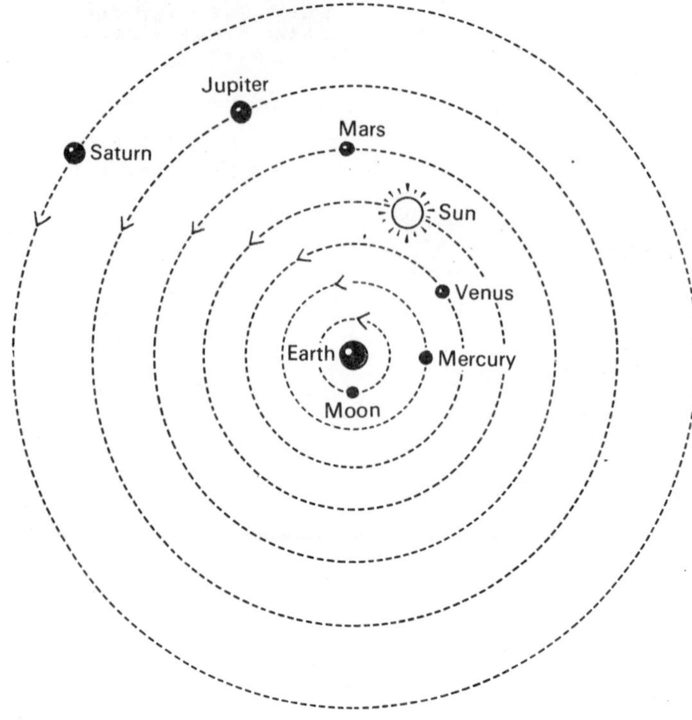

Figure 20 An early model of the Earth, Sun and planets.

single model like that of Figure 20 does not explain the *loops* in the paths of the planets, as seen against the background of stars. The astronomers of ancient Greece devised ways of keeping the Earth at the centre of the system, and yet moving the planets on circles so as to make their paths appear looped. These ways are very complicated. Fortunately, a little over 400 years ago, a Polish astronomer Nicolas Copernicus suggested that the *Sun* is at the centre of the system. With the Earth and the planets all circling the Sun. He suggested that the different planets were at different distances from the Sun, and that the further away from the Sun a star was, the more slowly it moved. Then the loops in the paths that the planets seemed to follow could be explained more simply than before.

As you may well imagine, Copernicus's suggestion caused a good deal of argument. Some of the best astronomers agreed with Copernicus immediately, but most educated men did not do so until the early seventeenth century.

THE MOTION OF THE EARTH

As explained, the Earth moves round the Sun. It does so once in about $365\frac{1}{4}$ days. The Earth also spins on its axis, roughly once per day. The axis of the Earth is at an angle of about $66\frac{1}{2}°$ to the plane of the orbit. This is all shown in Figure 21.

Perhaps you can see how this picture is Figure 18 turned inside out. Since we observe from the Earth, astronomers often prefer to use diagrams like 18, with the Earth at the centre, although of course they are not disagreeing with Copernicus when they do so.

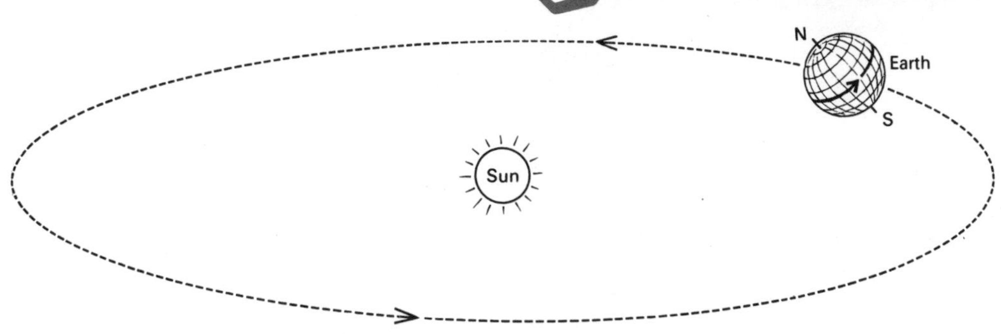

Figure 21 The Earth's path round the Sun.

THE SIZE OF THE SOLAR SYSTEM

Observation with a telescope, and careful thinking have helped man to learn much about the planets, their sizes, and their distances from the Sun. Try to construct a scale model of the solar system, or a part of it. The following table gives the information you need:

Planet	Distances from the Sun		Diameters–number of times as big as the Earth's
	Number of times as far as Earth	In millions of miles	
Mercury	0·4	36	0·39
Venus	0·7	67	0·96
Earth	1·0	93	1·00
Mars	1·5	142	0·53
Jupiter	5·2	483	10·9
Saturn	9·5	886	9·0
Uranus	19·2	1782	3·7
Neptune	30·1	2792	3·4
Pluto	39·5	3675	0·5 or 1·0

You will find it quite difficult to make a true scale model, but at least you will see that the distances are enormous!

TIME

The daily rotation of the Earth, measured by the sun, gives us our unit of time. Basically, a *day* is the interval between one *noon* and the next. It is 12 noon for any observer when the Sun passes most nearly overhead – that is, when the Sun is vertically above his north-south line – see Figure 22. (The vertical north-south plane in which the Sun lies at noon is called the **meridian**.) The day thus arrived at is then divided up into 24 hours, each hour is divided into 60 minutes, and each minute into 60 seconds. This explains how astronomy first gave us our units of time.

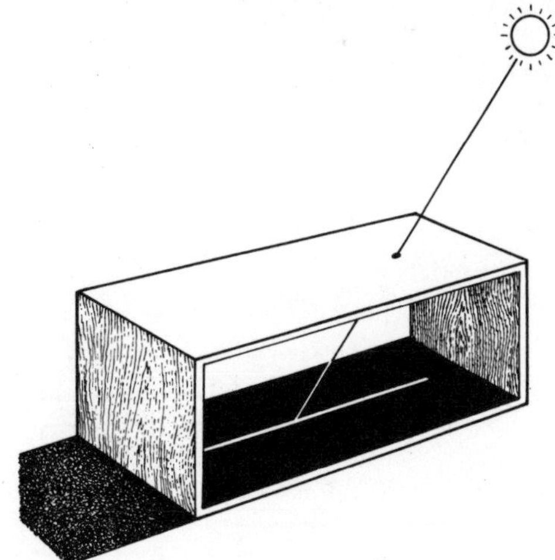

Figure 22 At 12 o'clock noon the spot of sunlight lies on the white north–south line marked on the box.

WORD LIST

axis **constellations** **meridian** **pole star**

QUESTIONS

1. Which two stars of the Plough are in line with the pole star? What other pairs of bright stars can you find that will serve as pointers of this sort, to help find the pole star?

2. Would the pattern of stars in the sky be so constant if there were stars very near to us, as well as far away?

3. Some constellations rise and set, like the sun. Are there any stars that are *always* visible from any place on the Earth?

4. Can you explain how the paths of the planets seem to be looped, when in reality they are not? (Assume that the planets, and the Earth, move in circles round the sun. Make use of a diagram.)

5. Can you invent a possible theory to account for different colours in the stars?

6. At roughly what time in history do you imagine that the phrase "Solar system" was first used?

7. A time exposure of the eastern horizon is taken just as Jupiter is rising. What would you expect the photograph to show?

8. From Sydney, Australia, the Sun is seen to rise at 6.45 a.m. north of east. What season of the year is it?

9. A Sussex schoolgirl spent the Christmas holidays in Scotland. What might she have noticed about the times of sunrise and sunset there?

10. Make a list of arguments for and against the probability of living things existing on Mars.

11. Draw diagrams to show how you think Venus would appear from Earth
   (a) when Venus and the Earth are on the same side of the Sun;
   (b) when Venus is on the far side of the Sun from the Earth, but not directly behind the Sun.

12. Would Jupiter, as seen through a telescope, show phases similar to the Moon and Venus? Explain.

13. Explain how you would use your knowledge of astronomy in order to find your way across unknown country at night without a compass.

4 TIME

Throughout our history man has had two obvious units of time, the day and the year. The day is easy to recognize because we experience daylight and darkness – as the Earth spins on its axis. The year also has always been easy to recognize because of the seasons. A day is the period of time for one complete rotation of the Earth, and the year is the time taken for the Earth to make one complete revolution around the Sun. It does this in *just* under 365¼ days.

Naturally enough then, men used first the day and second the year to measure the passing of time. For accurate time measurements during a day, each day has been divided by 24 to give us *hours*. The hours in turn are divided by 60 to give us *minutes* and these again by 60 to give *seconds*.

At any one spot on the Earth's surface when the sun is most nearly overhead, we call the time midday, 12 o'clock or 12 noon. The actual time as shown by a clock will be different in different parts of the world. When it is 12 noon in England, it will be *midnight* at the place on the opposite side of the Earth, in New Zealand.

In ancient times, before clocks were invented, man used sundials to measure time during the day. The earliest *mechanical* clocks were invented in Europe during the thirteenth century. They were used in churches to mark the times of services. People say there was a clock in Westminster in 1288. And if you go to Salisbury cathedral you will find a clock that dates from 1386.

Early clocks used weights to drive them. They had a weight tied on the end of a strong line, which was gradually pulled downwards by the Earth's pull of gravity (Figure 23). As it fell the weight worked the clock mechanism. And when the weight reached the bottom it had to be wound up again – like a "grandfather" clock but without a pendulum.

The **pendulum** was invented by Galileo in 1581. Galileo was then only 17. He was kneeling in the cathedral in Pisa watching the great cathedral lamp swing. Using the pulse in his own wrist to measure the time, he noted a surprising thing: the time of swing of the lamp did not alter. He wrote afterwards,

> "Thousands of times I have observed vibrations, especially in churches, where lamps, suspended by long cords, had been inadvertently set into motion . . . But I never dreamed of learning . . . (that each) would employ the same time in passing. . . ."

Thus Galileo discovered that a swinging pendulum would regularly "tick" away a unit of time. Even if the swing gradually died down the time would remain unaffected.

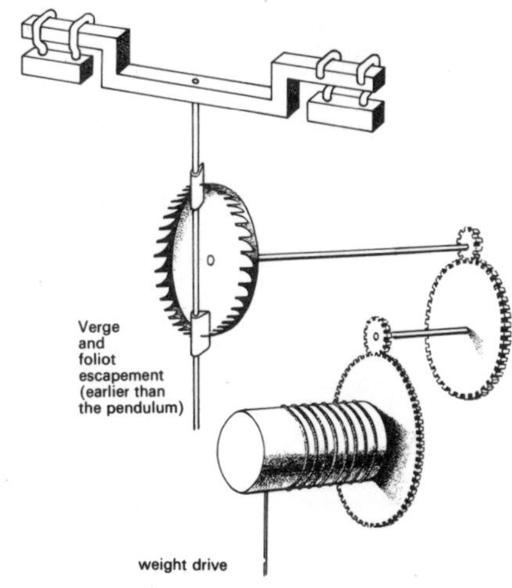

Figure 23 Weight-and-rope drive of early clocks.

Many types of clocks were invented based on the swinging pendulum. Only a very small amount of energy was needed to keep the pendulum swinging. A quite small weight attached to a string and being pulled down gradually by gravity was enough. Such pendulum clocks were much more accurate than earlier kinds. A "grandfather" clock has weights and a pendulum, but in many modern clocks the pendulum is kept swinging by means of a coiled spring.

Have a look inside a small household clock or watch. It does not have a pendulum. It has a "balance wheel", which swings to and fro. Electric clocks do not even need this. The regular waves of the alternating current mains supply keep them to time.

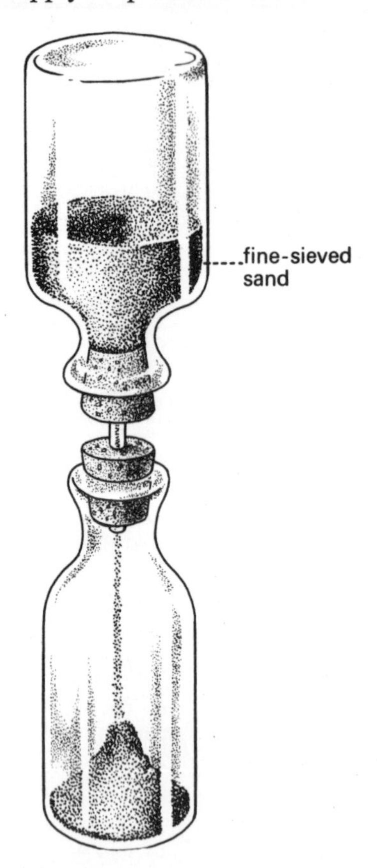

Figure 24 Hour-glass.

EXPERIMENT 1.

To make an "hour-glass". Join two small bottles by a glass tube passing through the cork of each. Nearly fill one bottle with sieved, dry sand. See if you can arrange the the size of the hole in the glass tube, so that the upper glass takes exactly one hour to empty. Figure 24 shows the details.

EXPERIMENT 2.

To learn something of the pendulum. Most schools have sets of cast-iron weights with a ring in each. Choose a 4 lb, 2 lb and 1 lb weight and hang each in turn from a hook in the ceiling on strong string as illustrated in Figure 25. See that the weight can do no damage if the thread breaks – have it a few inches above the bench or floor. Measure the length of the thread from the middle of the weight to the ceiling.

Draw the 1 lb weight back, let it go and find the number of times it swings to and fro in one minute. Now do this again but draw it back further and time it as before.

Now draw the weight back a *very little way* and time it as before.

Now put the 2 lb weight on, keeping the length of string the same, and repeat the tests. Then put the 4 lb weight on and repeat the tests.
Fill in a table like this.

Weight of pendulum	Length of pendulum	Number of swings per minute		
		First displacement	Larger displacement	Very small displacement
1 lb 2 lb 4 lb				

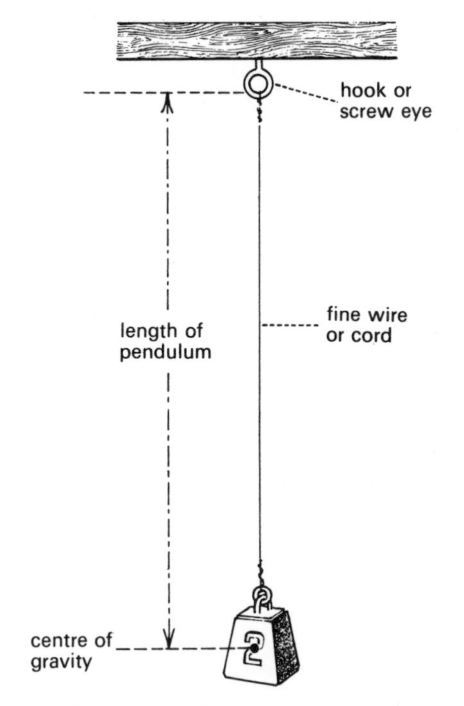

Figure 25 Simple pendulum.

Does the width of swing have any effect on the time the pendulum takes to swing? (Q.1).

Does the size of the weight have any effect? (Q.2).

EXPERIMENT 3.

Shorten the string and repeat the experiment with one of the weights. Does a pendulum swing faster or slower when you make it shorter?

EXPERIMENT 4.

To make a pendulum that beats "seconds". Try a string about one metre long to begin with, and test the number of swings in a minute. Keep altering the length until you obtain 60 swings per minute.

MAN ON THE EARTH

We know that the earth is many millions of years old. How would you try to work out how long man had been living on it? Your history book may go back quite a long way. It may tell you about the Egyptian and Babylonian civilizations in 3000 B.C. – 3 thousand years before the birth of Christ.

Even so man-like beings have lived on Earth for more than *1 million* years! This story was discovered by **archaeologists** who have to dig to find the remains of buildings, tools and so on. The further back they go in time the less complete the story is. In his early days man did not make many things or leave as much behind. He was a hunter, and did not build houses but sometimes sheltered in caves. Some of his story can be learned from pictures he drew on the cave walls. Stone implements have been found in caves and in the soil. We have been able to learn quite a lot about man by looking carefully at the soil and the rocks under it, and at the crust of the Earth.

See what you can find by digging a hole in your garden. In the garden of a house built where there was once an old boarding school, people found marbles, broken bottles, bricks and galvanized iron. This told something of the habits of those who lived there before. People have dug in many parts of the British Isles and found the foundations of buildings put up in Roman times, and evidence of man's activities in many earlier civilizations.

Figure 26 illustrates how records of the past are left behind under the ground. It is an imaginary diagram to show how the earth can contain all sorts of objects. These tell us much about the occupation of the area by man, hundreds, and even thousands of years ago.

The diagram shows part of the steep edge of the chalk South Downs, and some of the

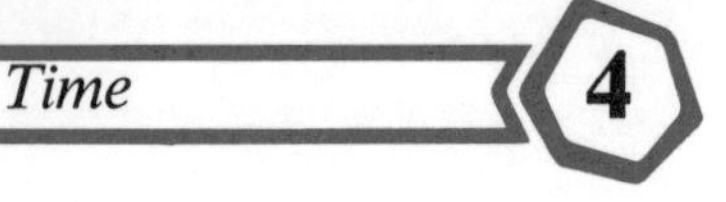

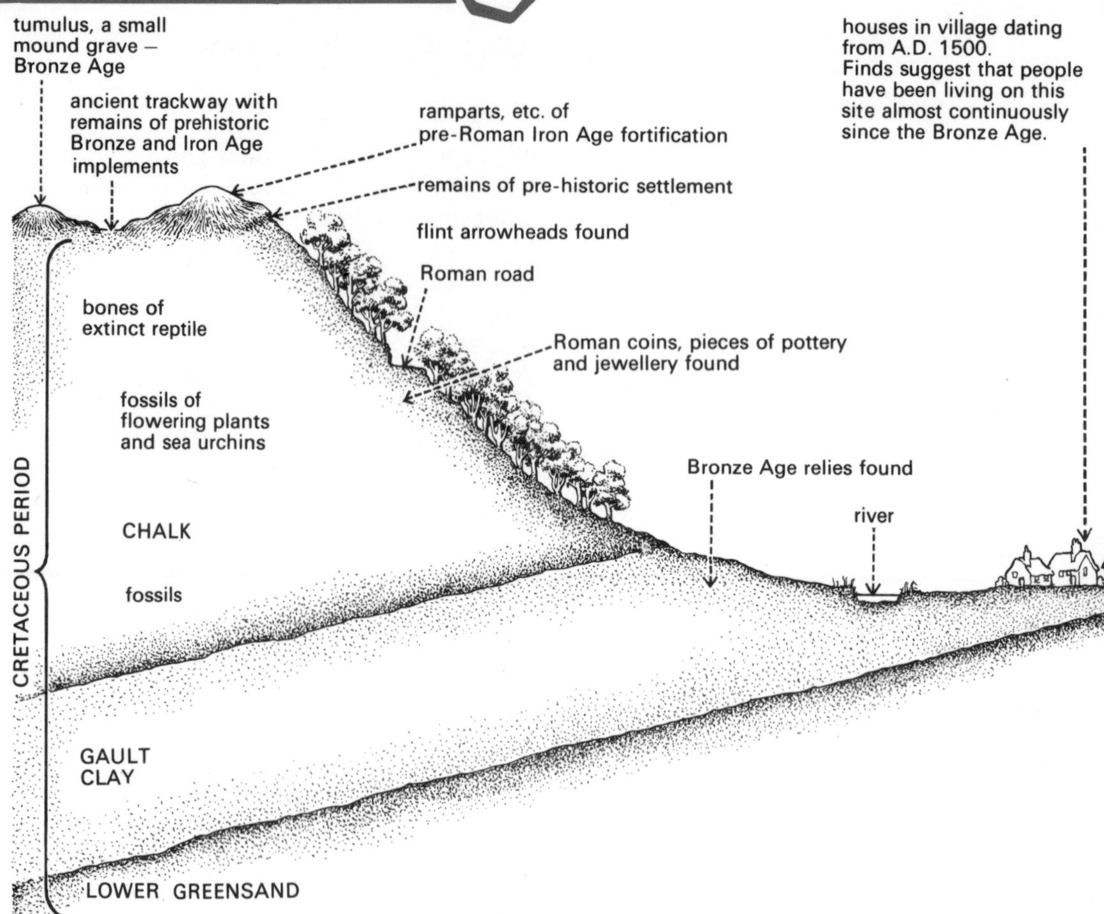

Figure 26 An imaginary section through part of the South Downs and the Weald, to show

clays and sands of the Weald. It is an area that has been lived in by many different races. Remains of their settlements, tools, pottery, and so on, can be seen both above and below the surface of the ground. Often a civilization has built on the foundations of an earlier one, and so the relics of the past sit on top of each other, the oldest ones at the bottom.

Beneath the relics of man's activities we can find evidence of earlier life – large reptiles which used to be hunted. There is evidence of the plants and small animals that lived whilst the rocks themselves were being formed under a sea, and which are preserved as fossils.

LIFE ON EARTH

Below the soil the rocks have been found to contain evidence of life that existed long before man. The hard parts of plants and animals, footprints and so on – known as fossils – have been found in the rocks. There may be many hundreds of layers of rock going down into the Earth's crust, each one older than the layer above it. Whereas the top few feet of soil teach us much about the last few thousand years, any information we get from these lower layers is very much further back in time. Traces of animals and plant life have been found under many thou-

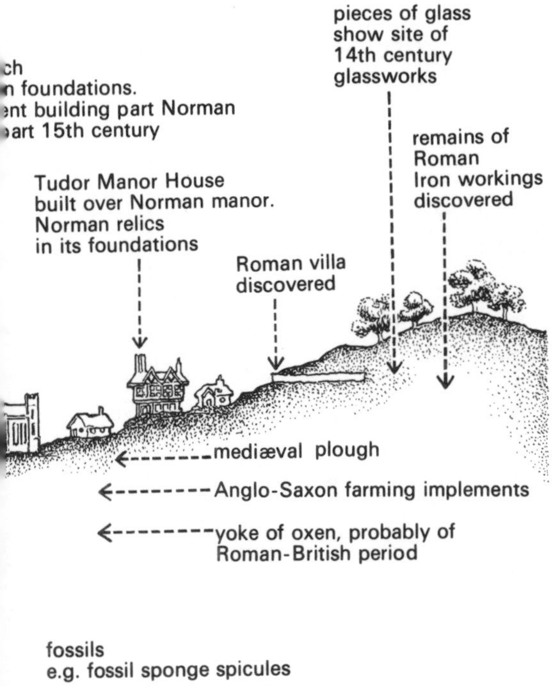

pieces of glass
show site of
14th century
glassworks

ch
n foundations.
ent building part Norman
art 15th century

remains of
Roman
Iron workings
discovered

Tudor Manor House
built over Norman manor.
Norman relics
in its foundations

Roman villa
discovered

mediæval plough

Anglo-Saxon farming implements

yoke of oxen, probably of
Roman-British period

fossils
e.g. fossil sponge spicules

land is a record of man's activities in the past.

sands of feet of solid rock. Such findings show us that life has been on Earth for a very long time, which is measured not only in thousands of years but in millions. The first evidence of abundant life is found in rocks 1,000 million years old (Figure 28).

PAST GEOGRAPHY OF THE EARTH

The historian works on documents like the ones you would find in a museum, and the archaeologist digs into the soil. The **geologist** goes even deeper into the earth and further back into history. He studies the rocks and minerals in the earth's solid crust. These provide him with various kinds of knowledge of past relationship between land and sea, past climates and ancient landforms. It has been possible to work out a series of pictures of what the earth's surface has looked like at intervals far back throughout its existence.

We could perhaps say that to a geologist minerals are letters, rocks are words and their arrangement in the earth is the story that he has to learn to read. You have a lot of work ahead before you will be able to read this by yourself but the story is a fascinating one.

THE AGE OF THE CONTINENTS

Geologists were the first scientists to discover the great age of the rocks of the earth's crust. One way they tried to do this was through studying the wearing down of the land by rivers.

Have you ever heard anyone say that something was "as old as the hills"? You may think of the hills as old but a geologist thinks they are really very young! Even so, it takes many years for the waters that run down them and the winds that blow upon them to wear them away. It has been possible to work out how fast they are being worn down. It was once calculated that the average for all the continents was about 1 foot every 9,000 years.

Another way to work out the ages of the continents is by measuring the total thicknesses of rocks forming them and attempting to work out how long they must have taken to build up. Anyone who has lived near a river that floods will know that in places several feet of mud or silt, perhaps even of sand or gravel, can pile up. This mud is called a **sediment**. In many cases, a thickness of several inches has been found inside houses!

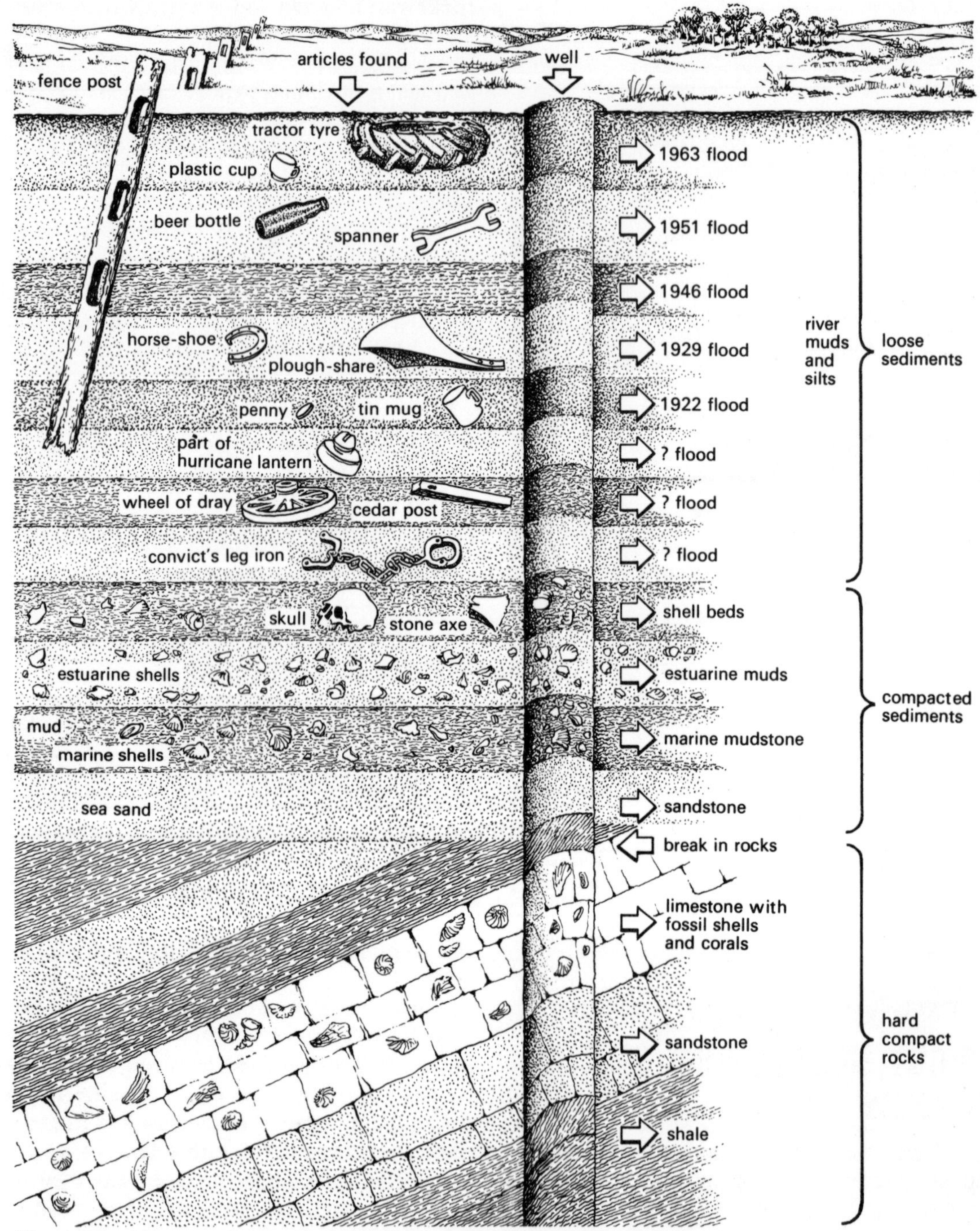

Figure 28 Showing how records of the past are kept by rocks. The objects have been found in wells, mines, and in sections of cliffs.

It is apparent that some beds of rock-forming material can be deposited in a few days, or a few hours, on the land and one would expect the same thing to happen under the sea. Sediments only form during floods though. In the Nile Delta they are believed to build up at the rate of about 3 feet per thousand years. Calculations on this basis, using thicknesses of sediments, concluded that there had been hundreds of millions of years since the beginning of what geologists have called **palaeozoic** times. Measurements of the radio-activity of some rocks lead to roughly the same result.

THE AGE OF THE OCEANS

One way of finding the age of the sea is to assume that the ocean waters were originally fresh and that all the salt was washed from the rocks and brought to it by rivers. Scientists know fairly accurately how much salt there is in the oceans today – that is, 12,600 million million tons! They have discovered that about 35 million tons of salt flow into the oceans each year. By dividing we get a figure of 360 million years for the age of the oceans. Some of the salt has been used over and over again, so we can be sure that the oceans are many times older than this. The oceans are, at the very least, hundreds of millions of years old.

THE AGE OF THE EARTH

Scientists think that the Earth started as a cool body, more or less as a collection of dust. The force of gravitation has pulled it all together into the rather solid body we know.

If you go down a mine you will find that the rocks get hotter and hotter; indeed, in some mines over a mile deep cold air has to be brought in so that men can work. In 1883, a great Irish scientist, Lord Kelvin, calculated that the Earth could not be more than 400 million years old but he later believed that the age was nearer to 20 million. Even his higher figure appeared to geologists to be much too small.

It was later discovered that heat is continually being supplied to the Earth by the breakdown of radio-active minerals. The discovery of radio-active minerals showed that Kelvin's calculation was wrong. We now think that the Earth itself is more than *4 thousand million* years old. This supply of heat is responsible for the inner part of the Earth no longer being cool.

THE AGE OF THE UNIVERSE

Let us leave the Earth and move on to the galaxies. Quite likely, the length of time they have been in existence is also enormous by our way of thinking about time.

Time and space are incredibly large; we cannot really grasp their limits, if indeed they have any. A million years is very short as far as the universe is concerned; yet to us, naturally, a million years seems like eternity.

Great galaxies form and stars develop, individual stars go through a "life cycle" and "die"; and so the contents of the universe keep on changing. Yet the normal life span of a star is several thousand million years!

Surprisingly enough, our own Sun is thought to be "middle aged" and will have burnt itself out within a few thousand million years. Our entire solar system could well break up into tiny particles. Does this worry us? Not at all, because a few thousand million years into the future is something we cannot even think of. The human race will probably be dead long before then! And to us even the future of a thousand years time is pretty uncertain.

EXPERIMENT 5.

To make a shadow-stick. On top of a vertical 3-foot post, nail a 1-foot square board horizontally. Drive a 6-inch peg into a hole at the centre of the board, as shown in Figure 29. Paint the peg and the board white. Cover them for weather protection when not in use.

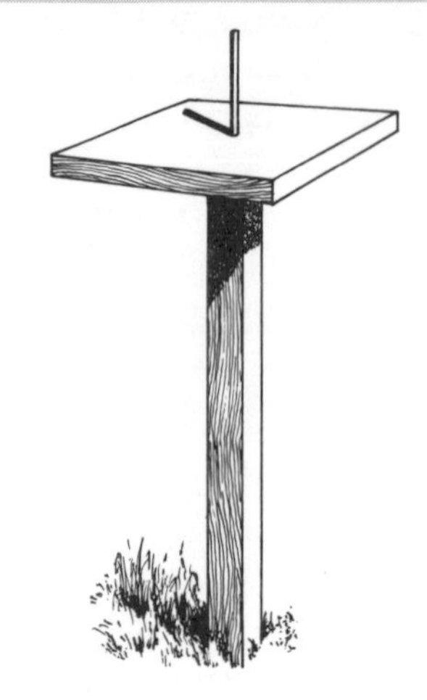

Figure 29 Shadow-stick on a post.

Things to do:

(a) Notice that at sunrise the shadow of the peg is long and pointing approximately west.

(b) As the Sun climbs higher the shadow swings to the north and gets shorter.

(c) At midday the shadow is shortest for the day.

(d) As the Sun sets in the west the shadow lengthens towards the east.

(e) As summer approaches, where does the sun rise? Where does it set? Is the shadow getting longer or shorter each day?

(f) As winter approaches how does the shadow behave?

(g) At midday on midsummer's day, midwinter's day and at the equinoxes – the days of equal dark and light – what do you notice about the length of the shadow?

WORD LIST

archaeologist **geologist** **palaeozoic** **pendulum** **sediment**

QUESTIONS

1. How would you measure the distance from your place in the class-room to the door?
2. How could you measure the distance from your home to the school?
3. How many "to-and-fro" swings of your "seconds" pendulum will it take before the hour-glass in Figure 24 completely empties?
4. If the Sun rises at 7 a.m. and sets at 5.15 p.m., how many hours of daylight have you?
5. In midwinter in the northern hemisphere how many hours of daylight would you get if you were at the North Pole?
6. If you were at the South Pole, at what time would the sun set in midsummer?

7. In what months of the year does the Sun appear to be overhead at the Equator?

8. Would the shadow-stick ever be without a shadow when the Sun was shining

(a) in London?
(b) at the South Pole?
(c) at the Equator?

9. What would you expect to find in the soil in your nearest park?

10. Where would you expect to find natural deposits of (a) gravel? (b) sand? (c) mud?

11. Suppose you are a farmer in the Fenland. Floods cover your farm about every 5 years and leave 6 inches of sand and mud behind each time. How long will it be before your 4 foot 6 inch fence will be covered?

12. Two inches of soil are taken every ten years from an area of country averaging two hundred feet above sea-level. How long will it be before the soil is lowered an average of 100 feet?

INDEX

Printed by A. Wheaton & Co., Exeter